Push and Pull

Lasean Ramirez

I0809785

Rosen REAL READERS

Rosen Classroom™
New York

A push moves something.

She pushes a wheelbarrow.

He pushes the cart.

A pull moves things, too.

The girl pulls a sled.

These kids move the rope.

Is it a push or a pull?

Words to Know

cart

rope

sled

wheelbarrow